Healing Song for the Inner Ear

Healing Song for the Inner Ear

Poems by **MICHAEL S. HARPER**

UNIVERSITY OF ILLINOIS PRESS Urbana and Chicago

Publication of this work was supported in part by grants from the National Endowment for the Arts and the Illinois Arts Council, a state agency.

Acknowledgments: Thanks to Yaddo, the John Simon Guggenheim Memorial Foundation, the Massachusetts Council on the Arts, and the National Endowment for the Arts, for support in the writing of many of these poems, and to the editors of the following periodicals in which some of these poems appeared.

The Massachusetts Review: "A Narrative of the Life and Times of John Coltrane: Played by Himself"; "Driving the Big Chrysler across the Country of My Birth"; "Goin' to the Territory"

The New York Times: "Stutterer"

American Rag: "Egyptology"

The Kenyon Review: "Memorial Meetings"; "News from Fort Ancient"; "Camp Story" (as "For My Father"); "Horse-Trading"

Black Scholar: "Paul Robeson"; "Homage to a Mean Monkey-Man"

The Michigan Quarterly Review: "In Hayden's Collage"

The Iowa Review: "The Body Polity"; "Double Elegy"

The Carleton Miscellany: "The Pen" (as "Hemp"); "Richard Yarde's Blues"; "Stepto's Veils"

Aura: "Filament"

Ploughshares: "Chief"; "The Drowning of the Facts of a Life"; "Myrdal's Sacred Flame"

Cincinnati Review: "Night Letter 1"; "Night Letter 2"

Field: "Hooking"; "It Takes a Helleva Nerve to Sell Water." (as "Inaugural Blues"); "The Loon"

The Georgia Review: "Dear Old Stockholm"

River Styx: "Chronicles"

Works in Progress: "Lawson's Return"

Graham House Review: "View from Mount Saint Helens"

Rhode Island Poems: "Battleground"

Chant of Saints (anthology): "The Militance of a Photograph in the Passbook of a Bantu under Detention"; "Peace on Earth"

Library of Congress Cataloging in Publication Data

Harper, Michael S., 1938–
    Healing song for the inner ear.

    I. Title.
PS3558.A6248H4   1984   811'.54   84-8633
ISBN 0-252-01128-7 (cloth)
ISBN 0-252-01099-X (paper)

Healing Song for the Inner Ear

Poems by **MICHAEL S. HARPER**

UNIVERSITY OF ILLINOIS PRESS   Urbana and Chicago

Publication of this work was supported in part by grants from the National Endowment for the Arts and the Illinois Arts Council, a state agency.

Acknowledgments: Thanks to Yaddo, the John Simon Guggenheim Memorial Foundation, the Massachusetts Council on the Arts, and the National Endowment for the Arts, for support in the writing of many of these poems, and to the editors of the following periodicals in which some of these poems appeared.

The Massachusetts Review: "A Narrative of the Life and Times of John Coltrane: Played by Himself"; "Driving the Big Chrysler across the Country of My Birth"; "Goin' to the Territory"

The New York Times: "Stutterer"

American Rag: "Egyptology"

The Kenyon Review: "Memorial Meetings"; "News from Fort Ancient"; "Camp Story" (as "For My Father"); "Horse-Trading"

Black Scholar: "Paul Robeson"; "Homage to a Mean Monkey-Man"

The Michigan Quarterly Review: "In Hayden's Collage"

The Iowa Review: "The Body Polity"; "Double Elegy"

The Carleton Miscellany: "The Pen" (as "Hemp"); "Richard Yarde's Blues"; "Stepto's Veils"

Aura: "Filament"

Ploughshares: "Chief"; "The Drowning of the Facts of a Life"; "Myrdal's Sacred Flame"

Cincinnati Review: "Night Letter 1"; "Night Letter 2"

Field: "Hooking"; "It Takes a Helleva Nerve to Sell Water." (as "Inaugural Blues"); "The Loon"

The Georgia Review: "Dear Old Stockholm"

River Styx: "Chronicles"

Works in Progress: "Lawson's Return"

Graham House Review: "View from Mount Saint Helens"

Rhode Island Poems: "Battleground"

Chant of Saints (anthology): "The Militance of a Photograph in the Passbook of a Bantu under Detention"; "Peace on Earth"

Library of Congress Cataloging in Publication Data

Harper, Michael S., 1938–
    Healing song for the inner ear.

    I. Title.
PS3558.A6248H4 1984   811'.54   84-8633
ISBN 0-252-01128-7 (cloth)
ISBN 0-252-01099-X (paper)

You are in the service
of the beloved
why are you hiding
—Rumi

For my parents:
Katherine Johnson Harper
Walter Warren Harper

'it's a wise blues
that knows its father'

Contents

memories are old identities
—Yeats

Every shut-eye ain't asleep
Every good-bye ain't gone
—folk saying

Re Persons I Knew

"Happy yes I am happy here,
  he told us; dying's not death. Do not grieve."

—Robert Hayden,
"Elegies for Paradise Valley"

Memorial Meetings

Clearing your throat
at the *high-falutin'* antics of friends,
in the first public light
(hidden confrontations, admissions,
confessions)—the jazz band
could not play, locked out of
reconstructed *Paradise* theatricals
in the old section of Detroit.
Sunday morning after peering at the Institute,
at the Detroit River,
suicides in the abstract,
the great bands of sing-me-downs at the *Koppin,*
squeezed in after a long line
to peep at Bessie, Leontyne,
and never on the same bill,
wondrous choral sections of the off-beat,
entries of the spiritual in the blues,
making the hi-tech engineers wince
in spectral tweetings, low exteriors.

A sound system is what you were,
silences and hesitations at the pitch
of character, the silent gesture,
and stories of the poor and elegant:

once on a train to New York,
the land's end of landscape
you could not see, the sheen
of water and the bridge at sunrise
catching you abreast of Monet and Rousseau,
nightmares of responsible obsession,
nightmares of the tears shed at our sins
against ourselves, no luminous heart
to wear beneath the surface pain
and our exterior joys.

You cried for us in the high-tea parlor
in the Calhoun living room in impeccable tears,
to singing and the score of Malcolm X
and the Egyptian rouge of Josephine Baker,
your favorite dictionary of the races,
dicta of the Chelsea Hotel and Uncle Crip,
murdered on the dance floor of the ghetto.

You stare down on us, face up,
on the divan of the Zulu King and Nefertiti,
but will not speak again,
the fires burning all night to your favorite
flowers, the scarf and blue pajamas
all packed up in incense and the reefer rose.

Your last tirade was at your barber,
who cut your locks so short
we could see your scalp,
and think of Fletcher Henderson,
and Duke, without the gray and cough
of the piano, the ugly world of vanity
in hormones and of the search for home.

Battleground

Driving up the highway
to Stillwater, and across
the staggered fields of upper
New York State, and into Vermont,
I think of you, sitting there in your bow
tie—at Bennington, perhaps, or Bread
Loaf—your pipe-stem easing of gauze,
the aromatic breaths of humidity
in the sky and your lungs and palate.

For once, the season, early August
a storm promised, one already broken
on the boughs of trees and power lines,
for once this season is over with the smoke
of your pyre; yet Miami, Chattanooga
wells up in the faces of the quaint
editorials, rehash of another query
into the destiny of man and country—
brainwashing and brandishing the sword
of Armageddon;
                    I stop at a simple shop
looking for the right map, the right postcard,
and find an old Sears catalogue,
with a pair of boots for sale, 1936, WPA
brogans, tally of the census-taker
and the wide-brimmed hat of John Brown—
speechmaker, and zealot, the books still say,
but he would rein down in the gallows
an invective the constitution never said
so well, and this invective I look for in battles,

Bennington, and once, a few days ago—years from now
and never ever forgotten, Ticonderoga, my father's
favorite battle—French and Indian, and English—
well, no more battles to fight. I pick up a skim
milked girl and her companion walking up the rim
of hill to the library, which is closed, and she

is carrying your book—unwritten even now, the music
of design, and vengeful paternity, and composition
written all over her face—passing for white,
in this black world, the right faces swing from boughs
again, trees, and lightning, and the gelatinous
wish of one more round of smoke, and the fire
of the word—pen and pencil, and the poems
you brought to life, and abandoned, somewhere,
in a room at Chelsea, or on the passageway
to any bookstore, where you peered for titles,
sacred fans, writing tablet which you gave
as baton, wishing well, talisman for the sacred
work of race and nation, and the word singing
everywhere, and nowhere, where no words are always
heard, gallows, and prisons and the great heart
of solitude, which resides in the trees, and clouds,
and in the earth, where the same old blessed roses
are laid down on your grave—and this call on the phone
of the ladybug, the dancer, in thoroughbred season.

The View from Mount Saint Helens

We picnicked on the Columbia River Gorge
on a splendid table of leaves,
olives, cheese, Rioja wine,
and talked of Ethiopia,
which Du Bois called Abyssinia
as a blessed namesake's child
is called "snowball,"
which is the word I name
as I look up at the mountain.

This was years ago, when I could
look down on the faces of the dead
above; I dream your son, Kevin,
looks down on us from his perch
above us, his face up to the ancestors
he could paint or collect
if he could leave the side of his mother,
in this life and in the life of Ethiopia.

The flying African would leap from the shores
of the continent called America,
though it was really only an island
in the Caribbean:
the text demanded the casirenas
be called cedars,
what a great poet called
the insulted landscape,
which is the breast of your forehead
now, so dense with frenesy
and greasepaint.

There is little comfort in the words
of a mountain: the Nez Perce would
climb Mount Saint Helens for vectors of meditation
and what they saw was what they lived.

I see you now in the busywork of healing
an old scar, perhaps in bed for a year
in paralysis, or painting in a mulch
for the cure to radiation, the bacteria
of the mind without vision.
                              Once you knit
for hours over my second living son,
Patrice, smoother than a seal or an orchid:
take him now into your heart for the mountain,
and the face looking up for us
who cannot see down, and touch the river
of the flying African in your bosom
for the husbanding of Abyssinia
to wash your wings.

Homage to a Mean Monkey-Man

A student called you a cross
between a monkey and a Pekinese
dog. I remember your asking
another brother what part of England
he came from: *Arkansaw*
was the retort, your tail taunting
the lion, your bite sharp,
well-placed and sexual.

When a librarian is black
and aiming for the classroom
he's death on women in the stacks,
your zipper uncocked,
your batting average over .300;
the story of your drive through Kentucky
after the Derby with some crooked jockeys
on two flat tires and a loaded .45
is a classic of the tall-tale tradition.

Your insurance policies are legion,
survivor of kidney transplant,
diabetic lover of bourbon,
all-night gambler at tonk and rummy.

Now is the time for thanks
when you pinned the ex-navy
officered president
against the mailroom wall
with assurance of death
if black folktales went untaught;
thanks for your threats to other librarians
gathering books you seldom read.
How did we know your bleeding
ulcers ran in the elevator to the stacks,
that bourbon killed the pain
so you could micturate in your office

hiding in the coat closet,
your fantasized blonde nurse
sopping up pee.

On a visit to Oakland Kaiser
you said you decided to live
when you saw your roommate's body
bounced and manhandled in a bag,
his penis tied up in a bow,
his unshut eyes clicking
to tremors of rigor mortis.
The man who came to visit
got shots of gold for his arthritis,
you talking of black gold
meaning white . . .
no need to fill in the epithet.

At a party over ping-pong
and the plan for the hostess,
her beady eyes focused on your belt
buckle, a black rodeo star with bullwhip
for a noose, you skunked
your opponents on whiskeyed
hypodermics of smut,
your whole football team
leaping the coach's wife,
for you'd seen it in your home
town in South Carolina,
and would never fly over it again.

You bought a kidney machine on insurance
to prove you could still love
any woman who asked for an inch,
a foot, a mile of blackstud
wordplay, and what you taught
was that you had to be killed to die.

Strapped to your machine
dialysis, green, black, and red
like the flag of freedom
you championed on your hybrid
stunted tree-climbing
to books in the stacks
of the slave trade,
you ran in the elevator
where the urge to piss
was confused in the woman
who abandoned you
never knowing the purity
of liver, spleen, kidney,
heavy yields at Richmond Shipyard.

A PS is in order:
remember your selling the entire
food supply in the Asian theater,
your European mess-orderly status
poking you to revolt
in stolen sacks of flour,
knives and forks
the East didn't need,
sheets and pillowcases,
powdered eggs and milk:
your court-martial
a citation of revenge,
little bad-talking Nat Turner
in a headrag of adjustment
to machines of praise,
your hollowed image of monkey
and dog, hind leg poised,
wetting any genteel tree,
if an any-colored woman was near.

Pacemaker

Pinned in dialysis
which stopped your heart
on the table
in the bright afternoon,
they cut you open like a butterfly
cast you could make in your sleep
in Minnesota,
and so I think of you cuddling
your son on a frigid
air force plane
from Fairbanks to Seattle
so they could operate
on his stomach
so he could eat.

How much of you died on that flight
and in the operating room
at the air force base
in your mackinaw and boots
and a plan to fish
and hunt on a squalid vacation.

You pulled your wagon,
an old beat-up,
brand-new, revivified
horse-trailer,
all over the country,
looking for your father
to forgive you
for stuttering at the table
before you could speak
when he demanded an oath of silence.

The broken lance and scalpel
cut into your breastbone
to start your heart,
your blood all clean

from the machine,
saving each penny
for retirement
in the house you built
in Florida.

I could ask
why Columbus, where I met
a girl from Fort Ancient,
Ohio, lost for a second
in the myth of an Indian
burial slope, why you married
a girl from Illinois
whose eyes and bosom
were as rich as the soil
she will inherit.

Buried in an army
settlement, not in her rich
familial loam, not with your son
who could not eat in Seattle.
Your heart never stopped fishing.

Double Elegy

Whatever city or country road
you two are on
there are nettles,
and the dark invisible
elements cling to your skin
though you do not cry
and you do not scratch
your arms at forty-five degree angles
as the landing point of a swan
in the Ohio, the Detroit River;

at the Paradise Theatre
you named the cellist
with the fanatical fingers
of the plumber, the exorcist,
and though the gimmickry at wrist
and kneecaps could lift the séance
table, your voice was real
in the gait and laughter of Uncle
Henry, who could dance on either
leg, wooden or real, to the sound
of the troop train, megaphone,
catching the fine pitch of a singer
on the athletic fields of Virginia.

At the Radisson Hotel,
we once took a fine angel
of the law to the convention center,
and put her down as an egret
in the subzero platform of a friend—
this is Minneapolis, the movies
are all of strangers, holding themselves
in the delicacy of treading water,
while they wait for the trumpet
of the 20th Century Limited
over the bluff or cranny.

You two men like to confront
the craters of history and spillage,
our natural infections of you
innoculating blankets and fur,
ethos of cadaver and sunflower.

I hold the dogwood blossom,
eat the pear, and watch the nettle
swim up in the pools
of the completed song
of Leadbelly and Little Crow
crooning the buffalo and horse
to the changes and the bridge
of a twelve-string guitar,
the melody of "Irene";
this is really goodbye—
I can see the precious stones
of embolism and consumption
on the platinum wires of the mouth:
in the flowing rivers, in the public baths
of Ohio and Michigan.

News from Fort Ancient

Don't ask me now, Jim Wright,
why this place comes to mind
but it is not arrowhead imagery
I look for, and the Indian burial mounds
embanked against the swivel and pull
of the Little Miami
won't bring you back to Ohioan
in this life, your soft glottals
and dirty jokes forever lost
in the atmosphere of swans
however dead and the oil leaks
from the cavity of the larynx
and lungs from which you sang.

You could cover it with platinum
but the sachel grew heavy
in translation: Chinese,
old German, a quaint, greasy Yiddish,
Spanish jazz, even from the mountains
of Cesar Vallejo,
even from the lips of Coltrane,
the breakaway backbone dice of Little Crow.

I knew a horse that did not sing
at the nearest corner post
in a field full of alfalfa;
he knew he didn't belong there
and so did I; I took the udder
of meat that hung from the mane
of Crazy Horse and made his enchantment,
an OM-2 automatic,
and the lake stood still in the early silt
of morning, without a fish, or a bird
in sight.
      You and Annie did walk
over a few blocks to the Y
to hear Etheridge and me read

in a blizzard—and you walked
back to the den of a world
out West; Cincinnati comes to mind
only because I went three deceptive
times to the bureau of health
to find out where a friend's mother was buried.

She died in 1937 and knew a few Cheyenne
in Oklahoma: when she picketed for social
justice she went to jail—the certificate
says she died of *tuberculosis of the hip,*
an impossible illness; at Hillcrest cemetery
the locks lock even before entrance,
and the phone rings to no answer even in the snow.

You know why I am standing on the Ohio
River, right next to an FM jazz station,
which ought to be on stilts, but is on a raft
bobbing on the windward side of a good restaurant.
I could see your suckhole if you held still
a little longer so we could build
your burial mound close enough to the edge
to be washed away forever.

In Hayden's Collage

Van Gogh would paint the landscape
green—or somber blue;
if you could see the weather
in Amsterdam in June, or August,
you'd cut your lobe too,
perhaps simply on heroin,
the best high in the world,
instead of the genius of sunflowers,
blossoming trees. The Japanese
bridge in Hiroshima,
precursor to the real impression,
modern life, goes to Windsor, Ontario,
or Jordan, or the Natchez
Trace. From this angle, earless,
a torsioned Django Rhinehart
accompanies Josephine. You know
those rainbow children couldn't
get along in this *ole worl'*.

Not over that troubled water;
and when the band would play once
too often in Arkansas, or Paris,
you'd cry because the sunset was too
bright to see the true colors,
the first hue, and so nearsighted
you had to touch the spiderman's
bouquet; you put your arcane colors
to the spatula and cook
to force the palate in the lion's
den—to find God in all the light
the paintbrush would let in—
the proper colors,
the corn, the wheat, the valley,
dike, the shadows, and the heart
of self—minnow of the universe,
your flaccid fishing pole,
pieced together, never broken, never end.

Ends of Autobiography

"Our work location was outside of Williamsburg. When I say that I MEAN WE WERE NOT ALLOWED TO DRIVE THROUGH THE TOWN to get to work assignments. There was a neighboring all-white camp that restored metropolitan Williamsburg. We worked on the beaches and environs landscaping—we really didn't give a damn—the city boys felt that it was their form of relief and so be it."

> —letter from my father on CCC, 1934, remembered on the 50th anniversary, "Since there were few licensed drivers I drove a dump truck for about 4 months—not a bargain—but better than mud."

Egyptology

The guide announces himself
in front of the sphinx,
the government price for the ticket,
a tip for me, the essence
of perfume to select with your
favorite drink, coffee tea cola;
it is extra for the mummy room
but I go on past the guide
to spot the hair, toes, and teeth
in the row of queens laid out,
the wall of the room like a tomb
with my polished sleeve its golden
covering, for I have a magic ring
from the Ashanti golden stool,
an American disquiet over the kingship
of Giza, the package flight to Luxor
on the drawing board.

We go back to the perfume:
the man's name is Ali,
we are the same color
with the same heroes,
my money, the essence of Chanel,
smeared out on my wrist
and fingers; I point the most
fragrant one toward his house of mirrors
and snap his picture,
promising a photo sent to
the name on the bottle,
which I promise to pick up.

The unity of the godhead,
the dynasties quivering on the pins
of the soldiers, always on alert
in the white blouses of tourists
as the great Nile flows by.

The essence of this museum
is an American on tour, each box
in a smaller box, the figurines
washed in the perfumes of the aged
guide, who says, "How many wives
do you have?"; he has two,
one for Sunday, one for Monday,
and a holiday the rest of the week,
all the time I have in Egypt.

Chronicles

"When I say me in a poem, it's someone else.
When I say somebody else, it might be me."
—Robert Frost

Correspondences, colleagues, collages,
your hearing aid finally off
in the British Museum.

I could tell you of the Asantehene
in his robes, offering me
gin and tonic,
or my influence on retrieval
of the Ashanti crown jewels,
but not now.

I write out my own forms
for the sacred *pass,* with photograph,
for the stacks where you have hidden,
burden and light of the fifteenth century,
the larched Italian dream of Paradise
adrift in the ear—

My own takes me to one vestibule
of my own forms, you've filled all the trivia
in for me, location and pedigree of school,
the universe of education; as I stand up
in my dark glasses, I take my photograph,
the same equipment as the *passbook*
which I would carry in Soweto,
where I was detained a year ago.

I get into the portals of the vast
literate holdings, behind the triplatch
of sacred doors, you my guide,
the great vistas of air in secret calm,
the dial or switch turned on, the quick prophetic
pace in the inner circles, auroral dark, or paradise or hell,
universal composition or translation.

I learn the prefix of the OED
as lens of polaroid,
never forgetting the nursemaid sentry
in unquenchable accent, behind the screen,
the slave-trade images, Constitution Hall,
all the Romantics spread out
in cabinets and vectors of display cage.

London Zoo

You take my triolet brood
to see the animals of our kingdom,
grandparents yourself, the years
of chivalry and maturation aglow,
rain or shine,

  then take them back
  to your wintry Regent's Park flat
  for snacks and dinner.

I speculate on losses, changes of venue,
changes of heart, Charlottesville,
the ex-president chairman asking questions
I can't answer; books you could have written
in your sleep—webs of students lined up all day
outside your spotless office

  I saw you slip up cavernous Horace-
  Mann in the early light
  preparing for the pride
  of semiliterate students,
  the world of World Poetry
  gathering at the corners of the pit,
  etchings of the tattered photographs.

"language is the only homeland." (Milosz)
Rotterdam: leading the world in shipping,

denying a visa to a Cuban exile
at Poetry International,

    Breytenbach receives the prize,
    in absentia, in glyphs of Dutch
    or Africaans.

There is a lovely zoo right here in walking distance—
    my own Olympus to take the sacred pose:

The children do grow up—so many students lost in 1976
    in the Soweto "riots" can't be found;
    over the borders of homelands
    the issues of the mind stick on the tongue.

I want to say goodbye in your retirement
with a short form of protest and the grace note
of the hearing aid turned down, not off.
You whispered to so many in the tired provinces
of the mind—were never lost in tinctures of the heart:

    Where is reality and justice
    if not in the mortar
    of the wall-less city, intuition,
    where tribesmen have the sacred
    golden stool where all sit down.

I shall remember your sound,
the cleared table, edible,
or palatable geometries,
the polity and power
of a photograph, of animals
in a broken cage,
the phosphorescent word,
the names of my children,
yours truly, the child alive in the man.

"Dear Old Stockholm"

for David Breskin

I was at a tribute to a great poet
when a composer friend and a great
musician said you'd limped
out of your plastic hip
to try your chops
on some tunes in the studio,
and limped out to the getaway
car that had broken
into slats of pavement
on Park Avenue
almost a decade ago,
and given up your horn.

I overlook the wonderful lakes
of your city,
and last night,
unbeknownst to you,
and uglied up with vague references
to your posturing offstage,
I heard an imitation of your name
on Swedish radio.

I remember hearing your tune
outside of Jefferson City
on the way to East St. Louis, Illinois;
you were right behind Illinois Jacquet
and that same solo on "Flying Home";
I was so glad to hear the four bars
you couldn't borrow from anyone,
having only discovered your dark self
on the elbows of a piano bar
in Brussels, or Copenhagen,
where the girls creamed at your profile
because you could dress.

You could play a game trumpeter,
Mr. Roosterman, in your royal
outfits, your off-minor changes
in the middle registers
and a sense of pace of the city
in the mind where your heart breaks into song.

Richard Yarde's Blues

"the corn is green," said the musician

Just off the platform, in populist invention,
and speaking impassionately of the underside
of Vachel Lindsay's "taking it to the people"
I cab uptown to the gallery where Richard
Yarde's black face envelopes between the phases
of the moon, black faces in the portrait gallery
on 57th Street, how many blocks from Bird,
how many blocks from the Savoy Dancers,
project of the tsetse fly, Achilles tendon:
"white folks don't want black faces staring
at them on their walls" is why the portraits
didn't sell; so we went across the street
to celebrate over dinner—boys on roller skates
pirouetted on the cobbled walks, on splintered
alleyways and grandees—and we toasted
to the artist.

        I could have asked him to recite
the famous epithets of Leadbelly, just off the chain
gang, and evil in tonalities of "Irene,"
or asked about the fingerings on the twelve-string
guitar, or why Charlie Christian isn't in the gallery,
but his blind father is—or what is musicianship
to intermediaries who teach the finger positions
to the poor, the popular.
                "Your pictures border
on the photographic," the reviewer said—
photography of the passbook and the blotter
where the heroes come to light; I leap upon
a subway train, another underground station,
on the way to Penn Station, tuxedo junction,
and of the painter's pride in Massachusetts.

Frederick Douglass did recruiting for the 54th
and you were born in Boston, one site of liberty,

the baritones and goose steps of other interior
wars, spectral landscapes, and the close quarters
of the colorist, the difficult edges of the nest,
maneuverings, and of the band on 5th Avenue.

Filament

Remember when you staggered up the veiled
streets of Iowa City, drunk, looking for no
one, with me behind you, sober, looking
for an excuse to get out of town?

I loved your broken jaw
and your broken dreams
building up as a cavity
of syllabic machine parts
your brother makes
when he cannot paint his pictures,
one resembling Mingus whose appetites
were bigger than the elevator
I got caught in with his sister,
six months pregnant, working in airmail,
and almost as tall as him.

I could invent three tales that would
bring him back as you brought Clifford
like crystal water, if I could remember
to see them, coming back to me in the trapdoor
of the ceiling of that elevator she shimmied
through, but he died in Mexico,
and his ashes fell in the same waters
my brother's did, after cremation,
and the flagship ceremony off the coast
of Long Beach has ruined my tunes.

Your light in the tip of a glass of water,
the frozen Spanish lips you taste
with Rioja wine, so cheap even a fool can drink:
play your horn in the throat of Clifford.

The Loon

The estate bird
sits on the water
outside my window;
if you watch long
enough you will see
her dive
from her canopy,
and in the understory
of the weather,
in trees,
beneath the surface,
you might see another
estate bird.

In this scene the call
goes out to the ground cover,
where you can lay your face,
unbroken by the ceremonial
tears of the funeral,
on ferns.

Oh deciduous pouch
of awful leaves
at a would-be cemetery,
listen to the loon.

You could dream conifers,
the deep roots of burrowing
animals and insects,
the opossum
drunk on his tail
hearing the interior voice
of secret soil layer
where we bury her.

"It Takes a Helleva Nerve to Sell Water."

Frederick Douglass never moved
to Washington in this address;
his statue is in Rochester,
in a city park,
a windbreak, my canopy.

In the 60s at LAX
he runs for office;
my brother's dark hand
stretches out in greeting—
no student of the Revolution,
he's selling water to the quake
victims in Santa Monica:
he's in his white uniform,
but nobody's buying
Arrowhead Spring Water!

He takes his hand
surrounded by security;
the eyes of the governor,
still as a pockmark
at Playa del Rey,
becomes the country's monogram,
markings of the movies,
a concertina of light.

I tell him how in 1934
they closed the WPA theater
midtown, Orson fell down
the trapdoor before Citizen
Kane, before black Macbeth uptown:
the black choral section stood
in a one-night stand,
sang spirituals below the poverty
line, below the stage threshold:
these blacks were thespians too,
Roosevelt loved the stage,

the New York Yankees came to power
in spring training; one night at the *Savoy*
Chick Webb battled Count to a standstill
on radio.

For the cameras my brother asks the governor
in his white uniform—will you govern for all
the people? He had given away his water
while others sold theirs, that he was a scout,
that the Lake is no stranger to him,
bowie knots and trails familiar as his tent.
We were tokens then, in shallow water,
integrating the camp swimming pool,
now embarrassed as headmasters on patrol.

There were redwoods; you could find snakes;
among the spruce and sycamores
the sansei boys were quick to break camp
selling all the water they could find
in the flooded pastures of their homeland
where we lived. Those who want crops
without digging in the ground
won't see the harvest in the movies.

Night Letter, I

I hear you curse your big sister, Eve,
her real name, and only a little biblical,
but what you kiss is her cheek
of an apple on the sly.
I thought of you on the mall
in Copenhagen, time zones
of amnesia brought me home
to black musicians I had loved,
a quintet arriving at the airport
as I flew to Stockholm: "what's happening, brother?"

Where is Stockholm?
That nation strikes on ubiquitous
May Day, birthday of Sterling Brown,
but when I was there spring
had just opened its vistas
so even the Lapps and their reindeer
could see through the dark to the light.

This is the land of the midnight sun;
the only one I really love
is Miles Davis, who's had an accident
and might not play again, but wrote
"Dear Old Stockholm"
for the old section of the city
where watermarks bank these buildings
as monuments to history and pain: St. George slew the Dragon:
The Jews of Europe sought refuge
in the underground station, the Castle Hotel,
so close to the Gestapo and troop-train centers
as to evade detection,
while Lapland, Norway, Denmark
fell into the pit of occupation,

and one old man, Gunnar Myrdal,
spoke of his pathetic service
at Princeton University

while his friends and colleagues perished
in the fires of a man-made sun.

I mention Miles Davis only because he is a great musician;
each time you sing in the middle registers

you recall him to your parents
who know the lore of the place
where his trumpet lies,
and since you are lucky
in inheritance of Druid, Viking transplant
and the Jewish specter of arena and the book
of law and therefore knowledge,
lucky you can hear the music
move your lips to the sun
shining everywhere in your name and namesakes.

Night Letter, II

          Last night I thought of you in your mother's arms.
I had heard a slender story of the crass folkways
in the Swedish countryside, jealousies of Norway
women, their noses so slender they speak as pipes
out of water, not wild rice, and not specters
of thin-beaked birds, not the profile of your mother.

I saw a half-Swedish fin of your father's birth
and came to the window of the picture
of a great old Swede named Carl Norberg
who could pick up a building
on the docks of San Francisco;

he was into his seventies when we met,
so gentle his touch—
so clear the lake rims of his eyes—
he could limp
from doing the work of two men
for a whole decade
in compensation
after a load of freight
fell on his friend.

Now I am in the Hotel Diplomat in Stockholm,
window of the midnight sun; some clear day
you will look out over the fjord
of this world and see the spring nettles
which make the first soup of your teething.
We will add the spring chicken of your gums
and a few *cloudberries* from the ladle of cream
to fatten up your cheeks and ankles.

I remember a discussion on ethnicity
in the town of Olivia,
a dirty joke from the past
which came from Poland
or a Latvian farm in the north:

36

here is drink and steamed fish
and a basket of wool
groomed for the last family blanket.

I wish you a comforter in the names of your family.
Amidst the jet planes and foolish trinkets
of youth you will hear a black music
of the past; there is little light
in the future without a sense of your loss,
ancestral and quiet as a cathedral,
cathedral of song and prayer
in the old country
not in Minnesota.

Harken the ovaries of desire;
swim the trails of tears in the good book
of the sperm whale, lake country
where the landscape is vast,
like "Dear Old Stockholm"
that Miles Davis played when I was a boy.

Cousins

"There's not much 'native' in North American gardens."

When he died on oxygen he died at home.
Everything is a weed of some kind,
a death route, an eastern ascent of Mount Everest,
two ways of making compost, exposed
to air, unexposed: he makes fertilizer.

On the day of storm the oak tree fell down;
the clock, losing its place on the wall,
because of the wind, ticked on the floor,
being useful; with no electricity the great maple
lies across the live wires; with no water except
the creek we count a dozen fallen trees.

Nothing blanched from previous years,
we eat from the freezer hardening off,
conditioning our young for the creek;
we planted castor beans for the varmints,
and, with a magnifying glass, counted
rings on the fallen oak.

          A bad year for deer in the reserve;
the friendly Indians taught the newcomers gardening:
"Jerusalem artichoke" is what came out, cousin
to sunflowers, roots that everyone ate,
in the free market, following the sun.

In the far reaches
of the family garden are perennials—it is market day—
they hold their own.
          You can eat it raw, fry, boil
unpeeled, for the "green eyes" adapt to the weather;
in a potato sack, with punched holes, you can store
in the root cellar.

The troublesome stakes are resistant to "tobacco mosaic";
smokers are not allowed in the garden. Your green eyes,

which match the marigold plants, keep insects away.
On the fence posts are birds' nests; in about half
the milk cartons are wrens, and they eat bugs.

Your father believed in clean air. When he welded
the metal sheets in the Brooklyn Navy Yard
he had a good name, though his lungs went flat
(on Roosevelt, his other good name)
in his native Algonquin, the language all natives
could speak from Maryland to the Saint Lawrence Waterway.

The best of the fallen trees are hardwood,
good for burning, a hot flame, warmth
from the belly of the garden:

Camp Story

I look over the old photos
for the US Hotel fire,
1900 Saratoga Springs,
where your grandfather
was chef on loan
from Catskill
where you were born.

The grapes from his arbor
sing in my mouth:
the smoke from the trestle
of his backyard,
the engine so close
to the bedroom
I can almost touch it,
make bricks from the yards
of perfection,
the clear puddles from the Hudson River,
where you would make change
at the dayline,
keep the change from the five
Jackleg Diamonds would leave
on the counter top or the stool.

Where is the CCC camp
you labored in
to send the money home to the family,
giving up your scholarship
so you could save the family
homestead from the banks of the river.

All across America the refugees
find homes in these camps
and are made to eat
at a table of liberty
you could have had

if you could not spell
or count, or keep time.

I see you, silent, wordfully
talking to my brother, Jonathan,
as he labors on the chromatic
respirator; you kiss his brown
temple where his helmet left
a slight depression
near a neat line of stitches
at the back of his skull.

As he twitches to chemicals
the Asian nurses catheter
into the cavities and caves
of his throat and lungs:
the doctor repeats the story
of his chances.

The Drowning of the Facts of a Life

Who knows why we talk of death
this evening, warm beyond the measure
of breath; it will be cool tomorrow
for in the waters off Long Beach
my brother's ashes still collect
the flowers of my mother and father,
my sister dropped in the vase
of a face they made of old places,
the text of water.

Tonight we talk of losses in the word
and go on drowning in acts of faith
knowing so little of humility,
less of the body,
which will die in the mouth of reality.

This foolish talk in a country
that cannot pronounce napalm
or find a path to a pool of irises
or the head of a rose.

My brother was such a flower;
he would spring into my path
on a subway train, above the ground
now, on the way home from school,
letting the swift doors pinch
his fingers of books and records,
house supplies from the corner market,
as he leaped back to the station
platform, crying his pleasure
to his brother,
who was on the train . . .
getting off at next exit
to look for him.

This is how we make our way home:
Each day when the Amtrak express

on the northeast corridor
takes my heritage from Boston
to the everglades of Maryland,
I think of the boy who sat
on the platform in the Canarsie,
on the uneven projects of New Lots
Avenue, BMT:

he was so small he could slip
through the swinging chains
of the express train
on the Williamsburg Bridge,
and not get touched by the third rail,
the chain link fencing of the accordion
swiveling to the swing and curses
of the motorman.

A fortnight my brother lay in coma,
his broken pate and helmet
in a shopping bag of effects,
his torn-off clothes and spattering
coins, the keys to the golden Yamaha—
with remnants of pavement in his scalp,
the trace of jacket laid under his head,
the black Continental idling
at anchor with the infinite,
the same black ice of the subway.

I came to chant over his fungus-
eaten flesh, allergic to his own
sweat, sweeter than the women
and children collecting
in caravan behind him; the Oriental
nurses, so trained in the cadence
of thermometer and brain scan,
came in their green bracelets
and uniforms to relieve him—

a catheter of extract
makes the pomade of his hair
disappear, for his lips twitch
in remembrance at impact,
rage at the power of love,
the welcome table and tabernacle
for his broken shoes and helmet.

Ponder the spent name of Jonathan,
apple and brother in the next
world, where the sacred text
of survival is buried in the bosom
of a child, radiated
in moonlight forever.
I touch the clean nostril
of the body in his mechanical
breathing, no chant sound enough
to lift him from the rest
of contraption
to the syncopated dance of his name.

Goin' to the Territory

"This liberating vision in Ellison's work reveals at least four major organizing impulses, four intermingled disciplining strategies for divining order in the experience he knows and for converting that experience into potent symbolic action: the *syncretic* impulse in his 'passion to link together all I loved within the Negro community and all those things I left in the world which lay beyond'; the *celebratory* impulse to explore 'the full range of American Negro humanity' and to affirm the attitudes and values which gives Afro-American life 'its sense of wholeness and which render it bearable and human, and when measured by our own terms, desirable'; the *dialectical* impulse behind his 'ceaseless questioning of those formulas through which historians, politicians, sociologists, and an older generation of Negro leaders and writers—those of the so-called "Negro Renaissance"—had evolved to describe my group's identity, its predicament, its fate and its relation to the larger society and the culture which we share'; and finally the *demiurgic* impulse to seek cultural power and personal freedom through art, to propose 'an idea of human versatility and possibility which went against the barbs or over the palings of almost every fence which those who controlled social and political power had erected to restrict our roles in the life of the country,' and so dominate reality by a willed projection of cultural personality nourished on the highly developed enemies and on the 'Yearning to make any- and everything of quality Negro American; to appropriate it, possess it, recreate it in our own group and individual images.' "

—John W. Wright, "Dedicated Dreamer,
Consecrated Acts: Shadowing Ellison"

The Hawk Tradition

Embouchures of a Photo
Not Taken of Coleman Hawkins

This is not a poem about flying
in the wrong direction:
into the sun no shadow
appears on the ground;
up in the clouds
a man in middle age
walks into the Missouri River
not far from St. Joe.

Why mention the Pony Express
as umbrella, a swift pinto horse
manacled in hurricanes of dance;
he rides in the eye of storm,
his echo glissing neither
nameless nor without displacement.

His arms around a Lady,
pressed trousers 'round his armpits,
his roostered shirtfront perfect
before the band; her earthy toothbrush
sings up-front of Hawk's solo:
this photo's familial with information:
Remember the river; the Pony Express:
his relatives know each place where his songs
bristle, where his name dances on water,
the back of any swift horse.

Paul Robeson

I find nothing of your face
in thick dull quiet of this airport
but I can feel your shucked
heartbeat in the record jacket
wrinkled in briefcase
where one hides one's clothes.

Stories huddle in curls
of hair whispering across
alleyways, dives,
your missing fingernails,
and last night I saw photos
of your mother transfixing
your pious father in you,
her sight failed on broken
bodies of song lifting curtains
in a small walk-up in London, NW3.

The tea drunk in London, in 1925,
holds one hand of a seven-year-old
refugee girl from Austria,
because it is a gift
sweetened with warm milk,
all she has in the world to give
in a hotel lobby;
I look through tea leaves now,
waiting for America to speak
on a summer's day on the Parkway,
your flanks oiled for the arena
of Franklin Institute
where your athletic letters burn in song.

"All I have is a voice,"
you may have said
to the federal agents
dovetailing in picket lines
at your front door,

low notes would crack
tiny pockets of air
in a steam engine backing up
over the dime you laid on a hot
rail in July 1911.

A man I loved flew from a small
Wisconsin town to Chicago
in a hospital ambulance,
his ticker-taped heartbeats
fluttering as you called his name;
banners in the country
ask for breath of your broad brow;
each airport landing strip tars itself
as gold you have given
blackens in bell-chapels:
little girl with milk
for your cup of tea
is mapping our family,
toasting flattened coins
you rolled down one street
bearing your name in Philadelphia
your countrymen visit
your gravesite, any airport
flown into, or away. America
is filling a deep river
in a milky sky.

Chief

In the year of the blizzard
in the month of February
I have traipsed up the middle
of Lexington Avenue, a spectacular
middle passage in the snow
to my own poetry reading:
James Wright, Philip Levine,
each having written about a horse,
neither a hero of myth
nor witness to history alone,
nor a palomino looking for a drink.

I could be water, or fire,
and on earth, which is covered with snow,
there is a bar where the air is filled with snow:
the air from my lungs billows in the fog
of my own friendly breath
as I walk down into the subway
into a labyrinthine holiday of dreams
and a *Book of Nightmares*
which I carry under my arm
signed by the author, Galway Kinnell,
after his introduction of Etheridge Knight
and me, a high contrast in poetics,
and the politics of light, and the smell
of the one horse I did ride
in Central Park after a girl.

Chief is my hour and my dark horse:
he does not belong to me, or to Crazy Horse,
who was caught by a bullet or a noose
because he was too quick for the camera,
the transcendent Lakota, Enchanted One,
whose name leaps from enchantment
to a horse eating in the snow.
One searches for the meaning of the railroad,
and the buffalo, and the hidden names of the horse.

In a blizzard, under martial law, and alone
in Providence, holed up in one office on George Street,
no easy street, and no snowplow, and no horse
to tread the rudders of a delivery truck
on the milk route, or the ice-wagon of my childhood,
or the stubble at the end of my mistress's hand
in the Central Park waterway of the horse.
A mixture of oats and honey, raw carrot
and a moving-picture camera of children
riding in the snow. I have loved this image
of a horse running over the plains of Scott
Momaday's *Plainview: 1 & 2*
and the detention of a horse in a mindless barn
of a friend, and once for the ridden part
of a season of horse in a park
where no child was the air of a poetry
reading, or the middle passage of survival,
which put name on the horse,
a camera on the man who rides the image,
and a hero as a witness to the woman
who rides him.

Pullman Pass

He was eighty-seven
when I photographed
him, straight up
in the natural light
of his fifty-year
gold service Pullman's
pass, 20th Century Limited,
and claimed he was there
when Rockefeller and Vanderbilt
agreed on the merger
at the US Hotel
in Saratoga Springs;
he'd been a jockey then—
the Skidmore girls
would count the hairs
on his smooth skin
while he told them stories
in any direction or position.

He told this dime story
once about Rockefeller
giving out new dimes
in the parlour car
relaxing from his dinner.

"I'll put these with the others,"
Henry said to Rockefeller;
"How many of those do you have?"
and so Henry went back to his locker
and brought back a cigar
box with a rubber band around it,
and opened up the lid.

Rockefeller turned to his lawyer-
accountant and said to count
the dimes in the box
and write out the check

for the amount,
a dollar for a dime.

Henry had a soft voice;
he roadsided every cavern
and watering hole when he rode
on his pass;
                he bought his wife
a farm with that Rockefeller
check: $2600,
a lot of acreage
for a black man
who feigned reading and writing;
straight back, tall as an arrow,
and pretty walking out the US
Hotel, where he had friends.

Segregated then at the Hotel:
wouldn't let no white people work there.

Lawson's Return

"Everything we eat needs rice.
These supplies must reach the people."

In Colorado gully and far from the river
two old men were shot gathering gnarled
wood to make a stand for a lamp
during the blackout: the pageant
of the 442nd collecting at the fairgrounds
burns the incense of emperor
in civilian clothes in Washington.

Embouchures of another tongue,
"Swing Lo' Sweet Chariot," sung by Brother
Rayford to a worrisome teacher
whose kin worked in orchards
of orange, of watermelon,
stolen ricefields in L.A.

Sansei, who befriended me in Iowa,
married a soprano woman from Missouri,
forgot degrees while practicing "honey-
suckle rose" in the Tokyo Blues
of Horace Silver and the Laniers,
we got across the bridge to Portsmouth,
the broken grandstand
and the open freeway.

Horse-Trading

He was accomplished on eight instruments,
none of them the women he loved,
and his middle son changed his name
to his mother's
the result of a quarrel.

You cradled him in your uniform
cut down from your unit measure
of paratrooper's boots,
for you were not coming home
in your thin quarterback
arms you once had broken
in preseason scrimmage
so you did not go to high school
or sue, or break out of the *I Am
Movement* your mother ladled
on her Irish brow.

So what of your perfect pitch,
the prosody of a mixed marriage,
same formality and freedom,
your cocksmanlike posturing,
flat feet going nowhere
in the open field
except for the snowing over,
the blanket, the foxhole, the spun reeds:

Once you thought Madison Square Garden
was a real garden with roses;
saved by the bell
your father did not die for nothing.

Hooking

Just about ready for medicare
and limping on that bum leg
nobody'd know you could mix
fine woolens from Australia,
spot-dyed into songs of the knead—
hook your way to the carpeted
gallery of birds and flowers.
The oak leaf breaks into difficulties,
pansies, their simplicity of touch
even at the water's edge,
as close to where you were born
as Newfoundland—
                        your man's gone
fourteen years, and in six
days you'll be sixty-five,
                             running the best
kitchen in Saratoga,
                   forty pails
in the early light,
                grey hours
of days off where you sit over the burlap
backing of the great rugs you push
into deceits of gold, rouge, gabardine—

Your birthplace is so far north, eight
hours beyond St. John, you can't go home,
though your father sits in his blindness,
walking the caverns of the family house
alone in his deafness; even the phone
can't make him walk any faster than your hook.

I can't ask you whether some Spanish flu
in 1920 made you limp,
left you childless, but I know your brother
drowned, and that your husband could leap
into the eggs of the mosquito without a single

drink, hitch from the hooking eye
you made for him.
                Nothing stands up forever;
your cane hangs on the wall just by the stairs;
when you come down you lift it as staff
to the rich life you sustain—
                         the music of the race-
track is clear in the mist and humidity
of August—West House closes at Christmas,
and this year you have ten days without a single
break from the hook and pattern of the winter's
sun. East is the best house; the flowers
bend in fragrance of the feed you lay
out for the cardinal who stays all year.
Since the sea is your favorite image in handiwork
as thistle and harp of the seamstress,
haven of the great maps of the world,
right under your foot, the heart stamps upon us—
stump, the pulling out of mistakes,
in the candelabra of your hair.

Stepto's Veils

I'm not blaming anyone either,
but authorial control is a reality,
does lie within the nexus of race,
and elsewhere also; upstairs,
where the saints carouse, upper
registers of song, encounters
on the levee, and in the stratospheres
of Coleman Hawkins—broken on his own wings.
I love the landing of a crippled bird,
all by himself in any key,
the glittering keyboard of a cartoon
character's teeth scattered into a dice
game. The confrontations of the word
are like the grace notes, and if you add
a race ritual or two, no harm
in epiphanies, the private jokes of cages,
arena and the mask of minstrelsy,
folk songs underneath the stars.

You pull back the cotton batting
of the great traditions, such privacy
and showmanship not only on the baseball
field, or in the segregated corners
of the dance halls; I thought I saw you
in a cummerbund, tuxedo junction
and the white gloves of Bert Williams,
who used to court my grandmother
while riding horse down 5th Avenue,
same avenue our ancestors went down
going and coming from France.

I think of Thomas Jefferson's foray
into the black section of Marseilles,
storing up footnotes for the Louisiana
Purchase, and since land is personal
the myth of Haiti and the Citadel.
Which brings me to veils: the doctor

would sit in his armchair making notes
to the arpeggios of the word;
finding no text completely comfortable,
he shook out his spats, smoked his last
Benson & Hedges, checked the stairwell
where he kept his piece, then went out
on maneuvers in the midlands of the people.
The buildings there were less than grand;
there were holes in the canebrake,
but the doctor had good eyesight,
saw the swamp and campground, heard the music:
the trouble with this century is more than history;
as for intertextualities:
this year's for Charlie Parker,
born sixty years ago in August,
died my senior year in high school—
nobody knew his tunes where I ate my lunch
with the sansei boys just out of camp.

The Body Polity

A half-century ago the Scottsboro Boys
jackknifed into vectors of the runagate
dream, and not the dream of Anglican
vice, when act hid shadow, shadow act.

Decatur relatives and neighbors,
not too far from Chehaw Station and Tuskegee,
flight squadrons and turkey regiments
peopled medical corps, jim crow'd tuxedo junction.

I saw the oldest son of any slave hide his thought
in Latin-English treasury books of Apuleius,
saw the roots of Constitution and the family Bible,
tree and joist of history, and the self: democracy.

A sterling beacon tintype or a work song;
thumbed eight-ball English, elegiac blues, on any continental
    shelf.

The Pen

"The artifact is the completion of personality."

The Big E. is still making up
complexity;
               he can't be stolen
from—his long black tongue
isn't nearly as deadly
               as his memory
which is of the frontier,
the fiber and floor covering,
the blossom and elixir of bhang
and hashish, and the pen is quick:
the seeds are used as food for caged birds

and so the Big E. enjoys a shared delight,
a feast.

The Big E. don't like theft—
he got powerful arms, a scarred
eyelid, and a pocketknife
that has a fast safety and quick release—
it has a doubled-edged sword,
               it is as black
as gunpowder, as red as a hieroglyphic
rose; the Big E. is a gangplank
with nettles on either side
               the berry sweet
enough for the nightingale to eat,
jam of the crow.
               The Big E. has orchestration—
his patterns of the word fling out into destiny
as a prairie used to when the Indians
were called Kiowa, Crow, Dakota, Cheyenne.

The Big E. ain't in love with Indian-hating;
he don't like phony dance—he's got his problems
with terrain in Mississippi—
               the great slab

of stone on the Mississippi makes you swim—
The Big E. likes hawks;
                            he's got time for deer—
he can seed watermelon, pumpkins, cantaloupe—
he got problems with theft,
                            highway robbery—
his own name—and he likes the source
of things, deeds, and the snakeskin well-wrought
and finely earned; he likes the sentiment
of defanging—he got two teeth with poison
in between, got a hot, tested lip,
                            a sense of ease
at the break—he's got a tinker bell
likes radio equipment, got tapes in his closet,
old coats still in style from the haberdashery
shop—has a sense of honor on the dance floor.
don't step on nobody's feet, brings his own smoke,
can tan a hide, fish in the stream of the dream,
the big dream—looks for the possible in things
unwritten; and when it comes to rite, jokes, jokes bad!

"Goin' to the Territory"

> "The prayers of both could not be answered—
> that of neither has been answered fully."
> —A. Lincoln

Ethical schizophrenia you called it:
come back to haunt the cattle-drive,
Indians coming into blacktown
because it's home; your father's will
lies uncontested, his blood welling up in oil;
"Deep Second" hones its marks in Jimmy Rushing;
Charlie Christian's father leads the blind.

Such instruments arrange themselves
at Gettysburg, at Chickamauga;
the whites in Tulsa apologize
in the separate library,
all the books you dreamed of,
fairy tales and Satchmo jesting
to the Court of St. James,
infirmary is the saints already home.

The hip connected to the thigh
converges in tuberculosis; your mother's
knees spank the planks of rectory,
your father's image sanctified
in documents, in acts won out
on hallelujahs of "A" train,
nine Scottsboro Boys spun upward
over thresholds of Duke's dance.

Dance and mask collect their greasepaint,
idioms stand on bandstand, in stove-
pipe pants of a riverman, in gambling shoes,
his gold-toothed venom vexing sundown,
the choir at sunrise-service cleansing
a life on a jim crow funeral car.

The first true phrase sings out in barnyard;
the hunt in books for quail.

My Book on Trane

"I used to hate Philly, not to mention New York; then I heard McCoy was born there, met Trane there—damn, I got to resurrect my hate for that cracked bell, and love the music; we need a piano-player to be mayor of this city, any city in America, long as he has a left hand; I don't mean comping, making changes, and trying for chords, I mean a real left hand; McCoy, he's got a left hand, definitely a two-handed piano player; and by the way, brother, a spiritual family man, definitely a righteous bringer of dawn light; we call him December child around here, because he was born late in the year, an absolute blessing upon us."

—overheard on the street outside
Penn Station, December

Bandstand

Monk's dissonant hat
willing every change of direction;
all those influences in your head
touching the wrong target—
none of this recorded,
the ears of the kitchen painted black,
all the musicians in common clothes,
dressing for the ancestors.

You learned to appreciate the pews,
the cooling iron,
the cooling board where the bodies,
guns in the recording studios,
became the tuning forks,
meals eaten while running in place
for Mother and Dad
who could dance.

Arpeggios

Hawks and pigeons first
on the jacket leaving profiles
of pressed flowers
on conked hair;
favorite compositions, things
distinguished in the pennywhistles
of the prow
in the mines.

Even in Rio, Paris,
little tangible is edible
that doesn't choke in the gullet
of misery,
hungry men playing
for each other,
blocking out this criminal world.

Genius lost and found
on the corners of Soweto;
Miriam, alone in her palatial
campus suite, clicking the sermon,
Armageddon the village-veld.

Polls

Some bloods can't count and won't vote;
imagine Desmond ahead of Trane
on the wrong instrument.
—I'm not saying Desmond can't play—
but *Playboy* was embarrassed,
sounding like swing all over again:
whuhfolks creating jazz—best records in the world
being sold under the counter;
Miles's soundtrack for a movie
only ten inches wide.

Trane created a freak show;
everybody scared he wouldn't salute
the old musicians,
the women of salutation,
his mother, cousin, wife,
the best connections
from the kitchen to the best restaurants.

Some knew such playing
is possible
only when you're ready to die.

Most whites always keeping score,
making it too easy to find the way,
guaranteeing you'll never feel loss,
black and white on paper,
in the ground.

Solo

Only sweet in the middle registers,
the fluegelhorn making new band
music, each cadenza
his solo of spare parts.

Signing the contract, unhinged
in the voice box, each triplet
measured in uniformed police,
he prayed for the big horn of attention,
and Coltrane came.

This was no everyday event:
reports of madness
with too much technique
for the life force,
the flow tuned in and broken apart.

Infections of the middle ear
gave you the inflection
you couldn't hear,
patterns given in pleurisy,
each breath killing your timing
until you drowned,
went to drugs,
the iron body
with strings
solo.

Obscurity

When he lost his leg
above the knee
he wasn't drunk;
cold sober
and sweet in the cheeks,
his compositions
on FM radio
right next to his mouthpiece,
woodshedding, leading the war.

Then there was the year of bad
phrasing; another, content,
with short interludes
of playing too loud.

Most women couldn't stand it;
not *his* woman,
who thought Lester Young
was an excuse
for Coleman Hawkins,
two family names
on the same instrument.

Disc jockeys were favorable
after the leg was gone;
blind with diabetes,
still drinking *rooster red,*
he could come alive
in jam sessions
with another's mouthpiece—
his own in the woodshed
housing the wooden leg.

"Engagements"

To work steady you play the easy
tempos; drinks, on the starched
tab, are free; a flask hidden
from the cleaning lady.

Engraved by a club owner,
short on grit and sentiment,
he went sweet and lost his teeth
while still in his teens;
the roll of the bhang,
on Arabian paper,
couldn't save him,
stocking cap pulled down
on each player's ears.

Alive, on the tab,
and no credit for his song,
he was forced to mingle in the crowd,
some of the best-dressed
losers in the world.

There was smack:
oh the distances you could make up
in a hurry
with the proper bloodstream,
payback,
the cost of the song.

Rage at the hottest tempos,
or play slow.

Prestige

Label in a period,
electrode for a voice
only Tatum can afford to sing:
imagine Shearing trying to cut Bud,
even in blindness, and Bud,
unable to play anywhere—
everybody backing off his left hand,
his sitting upon it, the alcoves
full of amphitheaters
in his head.

"I could play organ,"
he would say on the train
going uptown—"like Fats,"
his adopted sisters
scrambling the Jesus ballads

the wisdom of knowing
he never said a mumbling word—

Rumors

When Miles smacked your face
for playing the right notes;
after the encounter, your solos
paralyzed the audience.

Left-handed players had no heart;
religion was an end-stopped
melody, *the* broken chariot.

Players from Philly,
afraid to come to New York—

your liberty bell splattered
on the *AME* congregation,
readers of music, composers
who wrote down the group-effort song.

Spirituals have nothing to do with the church choir;
you lived or died on your instrument,
you died or lived on your instrument.

Sugarloaf

Up-tempo ruined his style;
Trane would come in,
ruining the fabric
of swing, of bebop.

At the bridge Chambers would stop
humming in the high registers,
Philly Joe in the outhouse
kicking his traps,
one last exit blocked for Garland,
out-of-doors in block chords,
trying to double-clutch and catch up,
giving the finger to the engineers.

We are always our best audience,
resting on the breastbone
of each performance,
refusing, in greasepaint,
and monkey suits,
to entertain, the mask
on blonde fables at midnight,
without candlelight.

In Newport (Sweden was over)
there was only Japan,
the taste of Blue Note,
the only sheet music
you could read.

When you pay the heavy dues of practice
play through the pain;
the easy chops are for playing after the break,
nowhere to go but the ruined swoops
of the counterpuncher,
unwinding to cycles of Lester
leaping in waterfalls of addiction:
paychecks for the bills long past due.

Pulp Notes

Too small a boy to play up front
of the band, but learning,
"all the things you are," to be heard,
"now's the time," above the drums,
before that the tambourines,
the whole aisle of women
just behind the beat,
and me, opting for Brooklyn,
after the whole middle class
had split—my fingers,
had I been gifted for the keys,
would have had their bandages
in ivory,
the honed protection of melody—
all I had was strings.

Four-hour layover
in the sack with a gorgeous whistle,
the whole city of Detroit
blanketed with snow
and nobody mad,
not a soul on overtime,
the meters, measures of skin,
a booming business.

Though I hated clichés
I never learned to drive
like Peddiford,
his Indian face
the best reason only blacks
take pictures of blacks.

Smack took my wrists
but the blood wouldn't give up
until I developed cancer,
no musician's disease,

a string man raised on pigmeat
eating himself.

I dreamed myself
learning to play at my own
funeral, in dress pants,
pimping in the gallery,
leading the blind to the trough
where all could drink:
tinkering with homemade radios,
invited to concerts on campuses
where I was learning to read,
enough good music to play
in the bodies of the women
I came to know in the ballads,
forgetting how to keep myself alive.

My Book on Trane

for McCoy Tyner

Waiting in lineups
in the rain you hear cosmic
conversations, "how many feet
above sea level,"
as though you could sign up
to play with Trane in the back room.

"What's the point waiting
for the last set if you can't see,"
and you smiling, underage,
protected from the blonde waitresses,
your new wife chilled to the bone
adrift in the fog of this music.

Every fool thought Trane should be taller,
an oak standing in water in his alligator
shoes, nobody able to hear Jimmy above the deafening
timber of Elvin, always able to hear.

Sonny, "just out of retirement,"
traveling with barbells,
had to have somewhere to play;
Clifford's dead; Miles won't play
facing crowds, addicted to playing "live."
One night I thought I'd have to squash
my hero, a dime-sized table, him
with his cuffs in my drink, peering
into the blue-green waters of Hawaii,
off Broadway, the Black Hawk, in North Beach.

Aiisha's always prettier in the rain,
the music loudest outside
coming into the brake—
the smoke coming off Elvin
as he strides across the street
to a working phone,

just like jet lag:
you can't believe the arc of light
in plain sight:
waiting for the drum major
from Pontiac with his brothers,
the steam coming off his wet clothes
in droves.

Peace on Earth

"Greetings:

I have the honor to submit the following for your information and consideration: For the past eleven months the country has suffered a severe drought which has destroyed the harvest; killed cattle, sheep, and game in many districts. The poor facilities for transportation in some sections greatly embarrassed the efforts to forward relief in the form of provision. The lack of water was an aggravating form of suffering.

A number of our missionaries could not reach the seat of Conference which met in Bloemfontein, Orange Free State, in the end of November, 1912.

During the past year four of our most efficient elders have died, among them Rev. Henry C. Misikinya, a graduate of Wilberforce University. Two others withdrew under charges, and six were expelled—four natives and two colored—thereby decreasing our ministerial ranks by twelve, a serious loss to our working force.

This lay membership increased several hundred and the financial reports showed an increase over last year.

The attitude of Parliament toward the native and colored residents of the Union is reflected somewhat in the passing of a Bill prohibiting any European from selling or leasing any land to a colored or native person; or any colored or native person selling or leasing to a European; restricting travel; and prohibiting a non-resident in a location from remaining over twenty-four hours.

In several cases recently, municipalities have refused a church site to any religious body which does not have a European at its head. Several of our large congregations have been scattered thereby, notably Pretoria and Heidelburg in Transvaal. Pretoria paid over $300 in Dollar Money at the last Conference.

The care of all the churches under such conditions involves much visitation, and the encouragement of much expenditure.

I am earnestly endeavoring to serve our Lord and Church. I do not hesitate to confess my deep sense of need of your prayers for patience and perseverance, and above all, for the grace of God.

I am, my dear brethren,

Your fellow laborer,
J. Albert Johnson
South Africa, March, 1913"

"I ran, and my people ran behind me"

—Jim Thorpe
Stockholm, 1912

Stutterer

Protea Station, Soweto

No matter where he looks
he jumps to his own breath,
semiconscious in Xhosa
semiliterate in Afrikaans
news, his remembrance
of English editorials
he is forced to read.

His bamboo baton
rolls across the interrogation
table as disclaimer
after sessions at midnight.

Three kinds of explosives
line the flowchart nailed
on the bulletin board,
one photo of a pair
of miner's boots
itemizes devices
in heel and sole.

You can't call the consulate
secretary, or order lunch,
the briefcase search
is routine, its broken slats
exposed as film
in towers of light
over 16 June Soweto
in quest of development.

Fingers separate in linkage
of starter and fix;
a high-contrast print
like a summer's
day in wintry Jo'burg
rises to the top of a teacup

and the Major checks permits
for the Europeans as our escort
says "all Americans are non-
European in Soweto."

The Militance of a Photograph
in the Passbook of a Bantu
under Detention

Peace is the active presence of Justice.

The wrinkles on the brown face
of the carrying case
conform to the buttocks,
on which the streaks of water
from a five-gallon can
dribble on the tailfront
of the borrowed shirt
he would wear if he could
drain the pus from his swaddling
bandages, striations of skin
tunneling into the photograph.

This is no simple mug shot
of a runaway boy in a training
film, Soweto's pummeled wire,
though the turrets of light
glisten in smoke, the soft
coal hooding his platform
entrance, dull and quiet.

His father's miner's shoes
stand in puddles of polish,
the black soot baked
into images of brittle torso,
an inferno of bullets laid
out in a letter bomb,
the frontispiece of one sergeant-
major blackening his mustache.

On the drive to Evaton
a blank pass away from Sharpeville
where the freehold morgans
were bought by a black bishop

from Ontario, Canada, on a trek
northward from the Cape in 1908,
I speak to myself as the woman
riding in the backseat talks
of this day, her husband's
death, twenty-three years ago,
run over by an Afrikaner in the wrong
passing lane; the passbook on the shoulder
of the road leading to Evaton
is not the one I have in my hand,
and the photograph is not of my great-
grandfather, who set sail for Philadelphia
in the war year of 1916.
He did not want a reception, his letters
embarking on a platform at Queenstown
where his eloquence struck two Zulu warriors
pledged to die in the homelands
because they could not spin their own gold.

These threaded heads weigh down the ears
in design of the warrior, Shaka,
indifferent to the ruthless offerings
over the dead bodies of his wives,
childless in his campaigns with the British,
who sit on the ships of the Indian Ocean
each kraal shuddering near the borders;

her lips turn in profile
to the dust rising over a road
where his house once stood;
one could think of the women
carrying firewood as an etching
in remembrance to the silence,
commencing at Sharpeville,
but this is Evaton, where he would come
from across the galleyship of spears
turning in his robes to a bookmark;

it is a good book, the picture of words
in the gloss of a photograph,
the burned image of the man who wears
this image on the tongue of a child,
who might hold my hand
as we walk in late afternoon
into the predestined sun.

The press of wrinkles on the blanketed
voice of the man who took the train
from Johannesburg
is flattened in Cape Town,
and the history of this book
is on a trestle where Gandhi
worshipped in Natal,
and the Zulu lullaby
I cannot sing in Bantu
is this song in the body
of a passbook
and the book passes
into a shirt
and the back that wears it.

Myrdal's Sacred Flame

> "What is needed in our country is not an exchange of
> pathologies, but a change of the basis of society."
> —Ralph Ellison

You greet me as "brother,"
evocations of Sterling Brown
and Ralph Bunche
and Martin Luther King, Jr.,
who sat in your apartment
after the Nobel ceremonial
hectoring of Vietnam
and world order,
the great diameter of poverty.

Your radiant blue eyes
glisten in extremities
of labored breathing,
shuffling pace,
and when your children
surface on your face
you speak of a trip
across the north Atlantic
in wartime, and the occupation.

Your guilt and pathos
at Princeton and Harlem
remind me of "Dear Old Stockholm,"
the lyric tune of Miles Davis's
remembrance of the old section
of the city where you live.

We go up and down on the elevator
as porters, as redcaps
of the B & O
of Scottsboro.

You ask me what is wrong with mad
America, and what the blacks are thinking.

I think of Coltrane's homage
"Reverend King" and "Peace on Earth"
as feeble compositions
to the scale of mass disorder
with a peace prize
and a people's march on Washington.

King asked, on that last visit,
what he should do when he went home:
"follow your conscience,"
you said; Coretta nodded;
Reverend Abernathy took a favored
arm; the official chain link fence
of the Democratic Convention
collects as radiation
in the American compost pile.

We take a cab across the city
on your visit to Alva
in the hospital
repairing for a trip
to toast the Einstein prize;
you drop me at the Hotel Diplomat,
call me *brother*, your world poverty
manual of survival in my case:
the Reverend King comes back
in modulations of a spiritual,
"Go Down, Moses, way down in Egypt land"
as though the brackage
of a folk song and a spiritual
could resurrect the victory path
of the Olympic stadium
which Sweden built for the 1912 games—
                    "WE SHALL OVERCOME SOME DAY"
you were a boy then
listening to rummages of war
in the colonies of Europe.

I reminisce about our moving paces
of the brothers: Dr. Du Bois,
whose goatee and whiskers
were stroked while you talked
in his study in Atlanta,
though never invited to his home;
and Ralph Bunche who suntanned
on Long Island with your children
where he couldn't go in Washington,
in "Alabama"; what of the medals
of Jim Thorpe, why he lost them—
his black friends on and off
this international dilemma.

I see tourists
and the flags of Russia
on a cablegram from the President.

I thank you for the company,
and that abstract painting of you
at the Chrysler Building in New York.

You shuffle in the distance
of the evening traffic
with reading matter
for your lovely Alva
and a tattered copy of *Southern Road:*

I think of your soaked telegram
delivered at a tribute in the capitol,
Martin Luther King, Jr., local library,
in the rain: great friend and brother
in the movements of dilemmas
of the arms race and relations.

The meter of the taxi
runs into the night of Coltrane's

solo on " 'Round Midnight"
where the midnight sun will set in
"Dear Old Stockholm."

A Narrative of the Life and Times of John Coltrane: Played by Himself

Hamlet, North Carolina

I don't remember train whistles,
or corroding trestles of ice
seeping from the hangband,
vaulting northward in shining triplets,
but the feel of the reed on my tongue
haunts me even now, my incisors
pulled so the pain wouldn't lurk
on "Cousin Mary";

in High Point I stared
at the bus which took us to band
practice on Memorial Day;
I could hardly make out, in the mud,
placemarks, separations of skin
sketched in plates above the rear bumper.

Mama asked, "what's the difference
'tween North and South Carolina,"
a capella notes of our church choir
doping me into arpeggios,
into *sheets of sound* labeling me
into dissonance.

I never liked the photo taken with
Bird, Miles without sunglasses,
me in profile almost out of exposure:
these were my images of movement;
when I hear the sacred songs,
auras of my mother at the stove,
I play the blues:

what good does it do to complain:
one night I was playing with Bostic,
blacking out, coming alive only to melodies

where I could play my parts:
And then, on a train to Philly,
I sang "Naima" locking the door
without exit no matter what song
I sang; with remonstrations on the ceiling
of that same room I practiced in
on my back when too tired to stand,
I broke loose from crystalline habits
I thought would bring me that sound.

Driving the Big Chrysler
across the Country of My Birth

I would wait for the tunnels
to glide into overdrive,
the shanked curves glittering with
truck tires, the last four bars
of Clifford's solo on " 'Round Midnight"
somehow embossed on my memo stand.

Coming up the hill from Harrisburg,
I heard Elvin's magical voice
on the tynes of a bus going to Lexington;
McCoy my *spiritual anchor*—
his tonics bristling in solemn
gyrations of the left hand.

At a bus terminal waiting to be taken
to the cemetery, I thought of Lester
Young's Chinese face on a Christmas
card mailed to my house in Queens: Prez!
I saw him cry in joy as the recordings
Bird memorized in Missouri breaks
floated on Bessie's floodless hill:
Backwater Blues; I could never play
such sweetness again: Lady said Prez
was the closest she ever got to real
escort, him worrying who was behind
him in arcades memorizing his tunes.

Driving into this Wyoming sunset,
rehearsing my perfect foursome,
ordering our lives on off-days,
it's reported I'd gone out like Bird
recovering at Camarillo,
in an off-stage concert in L.A.

I never hear playbacks of that chorus
of plaints, Dolphy's love-filled echoings,
perhaps my mother's hands
calling me to breakfast, the Heath
Brothers, in triplicate, asking me to stand
in; when Miles smacked me for being *smacked
out* on "Woodn't You," I thought how many
tunes I'd forgotten in my suspension
on the pentatonic scale; my solos
shortened, when I joined Monk he drilled
black keys into registers of pain, joy
rekindled in McCoy's solo of "The Promise."

What does Detroit have to give my music
as elk-miles distance into shoal-lights,
dashes at sunrise over Oakland:
Elvin from Pontiac, McCoy from Philly,
Chambers from Detroit waltzing his bass.
I can never write a bar of this music
in this life chanting toward paradise
in this sunship from Motown.

Peace on Earth

Tunes come to me at morning
prayer, after flax sunflower
seeds jammed in a coffee can;

when we went to Japan
I prayed at the shrine
for the war dead broken
at Nagasaki;

the tears on the lip of my soprano
glistened in the sun.

In interviews
I talked about my music's
voice of praise to our oneness,

them getting caught up in techniques
of the electronic school

lifting us into assault;

in live sessions, without an audience
I see faces on the flues of the piano,

cymbals driving me into ecstacies on my knees,

the demonic angel, Elvin,
answering my prayers on African drum,

on *Spiritual*

and on *Reverend King*

we chanted his words
on the mountain, where the golden chalice
came in our darkness.

I pursued the songless sound
of embouchures on Parisian thoroughfares,

the coins spilling across the arched
balustrade against my feet;

no high as intense as possessions
given up in practice

where the scales came to my fingers

without deliverance,
the light always coming at 4 A.M.

Syeeda's "Song Flute" charts
my playing for the ancestors;

how could I do otherwise,

passing so quickly in this galaxy

there is no time for being

to be paid in acknowledgment;
all praise to the phrase brought to me:
salaams of becoming:
A LOVE SUPREME:

POETRY FROM ILLINOIS

History is Your Own Heartbeat
Michael S. Harper (1971)

The Foreclosure
Richard Emil Braun (1972)

The Scrawny Sonnets and Other
Narratives
Robert Bagg (1973)

The Creation Frame
Phyllis Thompson (1973)

To All Appearances: Poems New
and Selected
Josephine Miles (1974)

Nightmare Begins Responsibility
Michael S. Harper (1975)

The Black Hawk Songs
Michael Borich (1975)

The Wichita Poems
Michael Van Walleghen (1975)

Cumberland Station
Dave Smith (1977)

Tracking
Virginia R. Terris (1977)

Poems of the Two Worlds
Frederick Morgan (1977)

Images of Kin: New and Selected
Poems
Michael S. Harper (1977)

On Earth as It Is
Dan Masterson (1978)

Riversongs
Michael Anania (1978)

Goshawk, Antelope
Dave Smith (1979)

Death Mother and Other Poems
Frederick Morgan (1979)

Local Men
James Whitehead (1979)

Coming to Terms
Josephine Miles (1979)

Searching the Drowned Man
Sydney Lea (1980)

With Akhmatova at the Black
Gates
Stephen Berg (1981)

More Trouble with the Obvious
Michael Van Walleghen (1981)

Dream Flights
Dave Smith (1981)

The American Book of the Dead
Jim Barnes (1982)

Northbook
Frederick Morgan (1982)

The Floating Candles
Sydney Lea (1982)

Collected Poems, 1930–83
Josephine Miles (1983)

The River Painter
Emily Grosholz (1984)

The Passion of the Right-Angled
Man
T. R. Hummer (1984)

Healing Song for the Inner Ear
Michael S. Harper (1984)